TWO BILLION HEART BEATS

Learn to, Unconsciously, Make Every Second Count Proven Time Management Hacks For The Modern Age

Sensei Paul David

Copyright Page

Two Billion Heart Beats, by Sensei Paul David,
Copyright © 2021.

www.senseipublishing.com

@senseipublishing
#senseipublishing

Get/Share Our FREE All-Ages Mental Health Books Now!

FREE Self-Development Book for Every Family

senseiselfdevelopment.senseipublishing.com

Join Our Publishing Journey!

If you would like to receive FUTURE FREE BOOKS, and get to know us better, please click www.senseipublishing.com and join our newsletter by entering your email address in the pop-up box.

Follow Our Blog: senseipauldavid.ca

Follow/Like/Subscribe: Facebook, Instagram, YouTube: @senseipublishing

Scan the QR Code with your phone or tablet

to follow us on social media: Like / Subscribe / Follow

Thank You from The Author: Sensei Paul David

Before we dive in, I would like to thank you for picking up this book from among the many other similar books out there. Thank you for choosing to invest in my book. That means everything to me.

Now that you are here, I ask you to stick with me as we take your self-discovery journey together. I promise to make our time together valuable and worthwhile.

In the pages ahead, you will find some areas of information and practices more helpful than others - and that is great! I encourage you to apply what works best for you. You will benefit from the knowledge that you gain and the ensuing exciting transformation of character. Enjoy!

FOREWORD

The importance of living life with the consciousness that we have limited time to achieve all that we desire, cannot be overemphasized. In this short but educative book, Paul reminds us all about the benefits of living life with the consciousness that we only have around two billion heartbeats to make our lives worthwhile.

It is a beautiful journey that begins by awakening the consciousness of the readers concerning the limitation of time and offers tips that they can leverage to make the best out of their lives. Paul has always been committed to adding value to the lives of people through his well-researched and impressively written books.

Two Billion Heartbeats is a classical Paul project. He has somehow managed to turn a scary fact into an advantage. Any reader would enjoy this. This is more than a time-management book. It is a complete package that has the potential to transform every area of your life, by learning to make every second count. Indeed, it's a great day to be alive!

Contents

Introduction

If there is a mathematical formula that explains the relationship between life and time, it would be:

$$\textit{Effort x TIME / LIFE = Time Management}$$

This is a simple but powerful formula you should always remember, to keep you on your toes. The implication of this formula is that your life is your time, governed by how well you manage your time. You are not an immortal being, and you should never forget that. You don't have all the time in the world!

Time is not loyal to anyone. You cannot tell it to take a pause and wait for you while you do something frivolous. Every second counts, and you must make sure you are not wasting time. Whatever you do with your time, is what you do with your life. So, if you spend a large chunk of your time on video games, it implies that you are spending most part of your life playing games!

The solution to ensuring that you don't waste time is to employ time-management hacks. The good news is that you will find several useful and effective tactics in this book that can help you in this regard. These tips are deliberately simple and broken down in such a way that you can leverage them seamlessly.

This book is full of value from the first page to the last. So, it is best if you give it your full attention until the end. This journey has the potential to transform your life. Whatever improves your time-management skills would improve the quality of your life. Therefore, this is not a book you should read when you are distracted. Create time to study it, like an explorer digging into a gold mine. You can be certain that it would be worth your time.

Chapter One: Fear Or Motivation

Scientists have discovered that the average human heart rate is 60 to 70 beats per minute. If you consider the fact that life expectancy in the modern world is around 70 years, then that gives us around two billion heartbeats in all. This could either scare you or motivate you to make the most of your life. In this chapter, we will explore the implications of the fact that we have two billion heartbeats, as human beings.

The Implications Of Your Two Billion Heartbeats

The implication of 60 beats per minute is that you have one heartbeat per second.

Why should this matter to you? Below are what you can make of this fact:

You Must Make Every Second Of Your Life Count

As stated earlier, your life is your time, and your time is your life. Therefore, you cannot afford to waste any part of it. Once you waste sixty seconds, you have lost a minute, and the moment you lose sixty minutes, you have lost an hour. It goes on and on. A second is equivalent to a heartbeat. So, for every second wasted, it is a reduction to your two billion heartbeats. Guess what? It never stops counting down. This fact should not make you anxious or scared. Rather, it should inspire you to be more conscious of time.

You should never have a day you wake up without a plan to invest your time into something that will be worth it. This is why it is crucial that you have self-awareness at each point of your life.

Whenever you find yourself unwilling to push to do something productive that would add value to your life, remember that time is running out. While spending hours on social media checking irrelevant posts, time is ticking away. The periods you spend gossiping about others are also parts of your two billion heartbeats. Ensure that you are always on your toes to make every heartbeat count.

You Have A Deadline

Studies have proven that people work more effectively when they know they have a deadline. For example, a 2012 study on Time Pressure, Performance, and Productivity showed that deadlines can be used to boost the efficiency of individuals. This discovery is somewhat logical because we tend to work faster and smarter when we are under pressure to deliver a task at a particular time. When you are not under pressure, there is a tendency to be too relaxed, which leads to procrastination. It is not always a good mindset to think that you have time. It can make you lackadaisical and unproductive.

Due to the fact that you have two billion heartbeats to achieve all that you want to accomplish in life, it means you have a deadline. You need to convince yourself of this reality so that you don't allow yourself to be carried away at any time. This does not mean that you should spend every day of your life building a career. If that is how you go about your life, you are not really living. In the words of Hillary Clinton:

"Don't confuse having a career with having a life."

There should be periods you spend with your loved ones. Yet, everything should be planned out so that your commitment to your job does not affect your personal life and vice versa.

You Only Live Once

Your life as a human being is different from a computer game. In a computer game, the character often has more than one life. It is also possible to get extra lives by watching certain online adverts or meeting certain conditions. However, it is different for a human being. After your two billion heartbeats run out, that is the end! You cannot get extra lives anywhere! Even if you believe in miracles of people getting resurrected by a supernatural force, it rarely happens! Therefore, it will be too much of a gamble to waste your life, thinking you will somehow get an extra one.

You only live once. Therefore, whatever will matter to you at the end of your life should matter now. Think about how you want your life to be on your last day on earth. What legacy do you want to leave for your loved ones and people that have a similar career path? Start working towards that now! If you made a mistake in the early part of the day, don't wait until the next day before you correct it, unless that is the only way. Make amends, immediately, and start working towards your goals again.

No Time For Regrets

It is normal that you feel remorseful when you have done something wrong or you made a mistake that cost you or your loved ones dearly. Yet, you should always remember that crying and sobbing will never undo what has been done. Besides, the periods you spend berating yourself, will be deducted from your two billion heartbeats. So, it is best if you reduce the time spent on allowing yourself to be overwhelmed by negative emotions. The reality is that feeling of regret will not change anything. Instead, it will only make you waste time on something that will not add anything to your life.

Time is ticking away. Once you make a mistake, apologize to the concerned people as soon as possible. Forgive yourself, too, and start making plans regarding what you can do to move on. Of course, you should learn from your mistakes to ensure that you make better and quality decisions in the future. Still, you shouldn't give yourself the opportunity to spend time sulking or crying about something you cannot change. Life is too short to be spent on regrets. Move on as soon as possible. It might not be easy but that is the best option for you every time.

Enjoy Every Moment

The aim of reminding you that you have around two billion heartbeats is not to scare you. Rather, it is to help you to maximize every second. One of the ways you can go about this is to enjoy every moment. This does not mean that you should always be seeking fun and thrills. Instead, you should give your best to everything you do. Don't allow the thoughts of any other thing you need to do, to affect whatever you are doing at that moment. Engross yourself in every activity and enjoy the moment to the fullest.

Living life this way is called "mindfulness." Studies have proven that it contributes to the happiness of an individual who lives life this way. In a 2003 study, it was discovered that mindfulness produces the level of satisfaction necessary to have positive emotions. So, learn to stay in the moment. When you are working, give it your all. In the same way, when you are with your family and friends, let the moment engulf you. Laugh hard and play like it's your last moment on earth. The fact that you have limited time to live, should inspire you to make the best of every moment.

Chapter Two: Leveraging Goal Setting For Effectiveness

The fact that we have limited time to live on earth is an indication that we have a purpose to fulfill within that short time frame. Nobody gives you a deadline for the sake of it. Once you start living purposefully, you will start setting short and long-term goals that you want to achieve within a particular time frame. In this chapter, we will explore how you can do this effectively.

The Art And Practice Of Goal Setting

Goal setting is an art you need to master to ensure that you make every second count. It gives you a sense of purpose and urgency that drives you towards achieving a set target. Many studies have discovered that setting goals enhances the productivity of individuals that have this habit. For example, a 2009 study discovered that setting goals enhances the efficiency of employees.

Nonetheless, there are some crucial features that your goals should possess that will make them achievable. These ingredients include:

Definite

Due to the limitation of time, you cannot afford to go through life without specific goals. In fact, at the beginning of every year, you should have things you intend to achieve. This is what gives you the focus you need to thrive in life. When you don't have definite goals, everything looks hazy. You will feel that you have so many options but don't know what to do, which can lead to overthinking.

The truth is that life always presents us with several options in every area of our lives. There are many career paths you can delve into. Still, you have to pick a specific one that will help you to harness your strengths and minimize your weaknesses. Also, when you want to marry, you will have many people you can consider. Yet, you can only pick one person.

What helps you to ensure that you make the right choice, is when you know what you want. You should not pick a career just because your father or mother is an expert in that field. You might not have the attributes that made your parents successful in that career path. To avoid wasting time, ask yourself what you really want and set your heart to achieve it.

Measurable

One of the mistakes people make when they set goals is that their targets don't have parameters that can be used to evaluate them. This is wrong. Your goals should be measurable. They should have benchmarks that would make you know when you have achieved them. For example, you cannot just say that your goal or purpose is to have positive impacts on the lives of people.

It sounds like a noble cause, but you might not be able to achieve it when you don't have milestones that will help you know that you have attained the target. It is better if the goal is to feed five hundred orphans or sponsor five hundred orphans to school. These targets are specific and measurable. By the time you have sponsored 250 orphans to school, you can easily claim that you have achieved 50% of your target.

Whenever you set a goal, you should always ask yourself how you will know that you have achieved it. Don't just say that your aim is to succeed in your career. How do you define success? What are those parameters that give you the perception that you have succeeded in your career? It is your answers to these questions that determine whether your goals are achievable or not.

Attainable

The fact that your goal sounds fantastic doesn't mean that it is attainable. If every target is achievable, everyone would fulfill their dreams, but this is not usually the case. To avoid wasting time, you need to be sure from the beginning that your goal is achievable. This is not a self-confidence issue. The fact that you are confident in your ability to get something done, does not mean that you will accomplish it.

One of the factors that makes a goal unattainable is when you don't have an objective evaluation of what it will cost you. Every dream requires sacrifice and a certain state of mind to accomplish them. For example, if you want to become a medical doctor, you have to be comfortable with handling the human body and all that has to do with it. You must also be prepared to read a lot of books for a good period of your life.

The fact that you plan to save lives is not enough to make you a medical doctor. In the same way, if you want to be a real-estate tycoon, you must love structures and buildings. When your passion connects with the desire to make the needed sacrifices for your targets, the chances are high that you will achieve an objective.

Relevant

When setting a goal, you need to ask yourself how important it is for you to achieve it. If you don't have a strong passion for what you want to achieve, you might drop it along the way when the challenges and stress that come with it pops up. This is the reason many people have abandoned projects. For example, you cannot decide to get married when you are not willing to make compromises and sacrifices for your spouse and children.

It is when it really matters to you that you have a successful home that you will be willing to make those sacrifices and commitments. In the same way, if you want to sponsor five hundred orphans, you must be willing to ask yourself how important it is to you to achieve this. Is it a legacy you want to leave before your two billion heartbeats run out?

You need to ask yourself this critical question before you set out because you will face challenges. Some of the orphans might even be ingrates. They might not value your effort at the end of it all. If this happens, how would you feel? Will you still feel that you have done something worthwhile? You need to answer these questions so that you will not feel that you wasted your life on a cause that was never worth it in the first place.

Time Bound

The issue of time is the crux of this book. Therefore, it is not something that should be left out when discussing goal setting. We have established the fact that you don't have all the time in the world. Therefore, every goal you set must have a time frame. It is like giving yourself a deadline within the deadline life already gives you. You have to work with time when setting a short or long-term target.

If you cannot provide a convincing answer to the question regarding the time frame you need to accomplish a target, it is not yet an achievable aim. You should be able to tell when you will complete an objective, so that you can move on to the next one. If you want to sponsor five hundred orphans to school, you should be able to tell for how long you want to achieve this.

When you don't have a particular time you intend to accomplish something, there is a chance that you might not put in conscious effort to get it done. If you intend to educate five hundred orphans within ten years, you will plan for the feasibility of the project. You will think about how you will get funds and how you can find your target beneficiaries within that period.

Chapter Three: Eliminating Procrastination

In a world where you only have around two billion heartbeats in a lifetime, the worst thing you can do is to waste time because of procrastination. Procrastination should be a taboo in our world. Yet, this is a bad habit that many people possess. It is vital that you get rid of it to enhance your effectiveness and help you to make every second count. The tips below will help you in this regard:

Eat That Frog!

Of course, I am not referring to a literal frog here. In this context, a frog is that unpleasant task that you would rather not do but have to do. This is usually because it is challenging and would demand a lot of effort and attention. Don't make the mistake of avoiding this kind of task and starting with the easier ones. Usually, such tasks offer the greatest rewards.

This is usually the case in an exam. Most times, those tough questions that would demand more time and attention carry more marks. If a student should leave them behind and do the simpler ones that carry lesser marks first, there might not be enough time to do them eventually. Smart students deal with the more challenging questions that carry higher marks first before they attempt the simpler ones.

You should apply this same principle when working and solving a problem. Make up your mind to face your fear and start with the tougher tasks. Once you have completed them, you will have the impetus and enough left in the "tank" to accomplish the simpler ones. Let this be your default mode of thinking and you will notice that you are achieving more within the time you have.

Discover Your Peak Period

You need to be observant enough to discover yourself. You cannot afford to try to replicate the formula of others for success because it might not work for you. You are unique and you have to understand those characteristics that make you special and different, to make the most of your life. For example, there are people that work better when they are given a task in the early part of the day. On the other hand, some individuals are nocturnal – they are more productive towards the end of the day.

I once had a friend that sleeps for most parts of the afternoon and spends his nights working. It was strange to me, at first. When I couldn't take it anymore, I asked him why he had that kind of lifestyle. Then he explained to me that he needs the silence of the night to be efficient as a music producer. He understood what works for him and he designed his life to that effect. He didn't sleep in the night and work in the day like most people around him, and it was not an issue for him.

It is vital that you know the part of the day that gives you the focus and energy to deliver your best results, then tailor your career and tasks around that period. This should be the period of the day you carry out the most challenging tasks you have. You don't have to be like everyone else around you. Discover yourself and maximize your time, by designing your schedule, to suit your personality.

Focus On The Reward

As human beings, we are designed to drift towards pleasure and avoid pain. Yet, we cannot avoid pain. In fact, pain often leads to pleasure. For example, you might not enjoy it when you hit the gym regularly for your work out, but you will be glad that you did it eventually when you see how physically fit you are. The mistake many people make when working on a task is that they focus more on the sacrifice that they would need to give, instead of what they would get at the end of the day.

Of course, it is important that you think about what it takes to complete a project so that you can make adequate plans to complete it. Nonetheless, you should not let that thought fill your mind. Once you have made an objective evaluation of what you need to do to get a job done and you are convinced that you are capable, stop thinking about the stress involved.

From that point, let the reward you will get after you complete the task fill your mind. Fantasize about it and let it motivate you towards completing the task. Think about all the things you can buy with the money you get after finishing the contract. Olympic athletes use this technique to drive them towards getting a medal. It is called visualization. A 2003 study showed that this technique improves the ability of students to learn in the classroom.

Get Rid Of Distractions

You should not overestimate your ability to handle distractions. Before you start working, take out things that might distract you. If you know that you are usually tempted to check your social media page, keep your phone away from you, if possible, until you have accomplished the task. Distractions will make you do less, even when you have more time. So, it is best that you get rid of them. If you are embarking on a project that will need you to think a lot, it is best that you go somewhere you can be alone.

Your loved ones might not know that they are distracting you, sometimes. They just want your attention without realizing that it is hampering your productivity. Instead of snubbing them or speaking to them in ways you might regret later, avoid working where they are. This is crucial, especially if you are a remote worker. You don't have to work from home just because your work does not need you to be in an office. Your efficiency is the most important thing. So, if necessary, leave your home and go and work somewhere you can concentrate.

Be Accountable

If you notice that you have not been consistent and disciplined enough to do what you need to do on time, you can get the help of a "watchdog." A watchdog in this context, refers to someone that can question you and find out about your progress in a task. You don't have to go too far to find one. You can tell your spouse that you intend to complete a project on a particular day and tell him or her to find out whether you achieved your aim at the end of that day.

The fact that you know that he or she would ask you about your progress, might be all that you need to work faster. To make this more effective, empower the person to punish or reward you. You might tell your spouse that he or she should not allow you to watch your favorite TV show, unless you complete the task. This can be the extra motivation you need to complete your project, as fast as possible.

Chapter Four: Simplifying Challenging Tasks

One of the reasons people waste time is that they have not mastered the art of simplifying tasks. They spend precious time thinking about the enormity of the task, instead of actually working on it. This is also one of the reasons some people never make any attempt to achieve some targets. They just feel that it is too challenging for them. Meanwhile, it would have been easier if they learned to simplify the goal. In this chapter, we will explore how you can simplify tasks to save time.

The Art Of Chunking

You can simplify a challenging task by breaking it into smaller parts. It is called chunking. Instead of wasting time thinking about the difficulty of the task. Simply think about how you can do it bit by bit. This can be effective in achieving anything monumental. For example, if you want to write a book, start by breaking it into chapters. Act as though each chapter is a project. Do your findings for each chapter and break them into subheadings.

By the time you start working on each chapter, you will discover that you don't have the mental fatigue that comes with thinking about the whole book. If you have five days to complete the project, then, if you have ten chapters, work on two chapters per day. Knowing that you need to do two chapters daily makes you more relaxed and motivated, than when you focus on the fact that you need to work on ten chapters of a book.

Redefining A Task

You cannot underrate the psychological aspect of whatever you do. Your brain controls all your tasks, including your perspectives. Therefore, it is vital that you set your mind in such a way that it will look favorably on a task. Once you convince yourself that a task is too challenging, you will struggle to approach it. You will keep postponing it. Meanwhile, you are wasting time already. Instead of thinking about the difficulty of a project, redefine it.

For example, instead of thinking that a project is challenging, think about it as something that requires more skills or the right tools. Convince yourself that you simply need to find a more effective way to go about it. When you start creating these positive emotions, you might be surprised that you will actually find a way to accomplish the task in a faster and easier way. Remember that nothing gets done, until you try to do it.

Get Training

One of the ways to save time is to invest wisely in training. Don't deceive yourself. If you don't possess the skills required to carry out a task, you will waste time and effort on it. You might eventually find a way to do it but you would waste a lot of time doing so. Instead of experimenting, find someone that can train you, so that you can be more effective. In the modern world, there are many useful materials online that can help you to improve your skills, in many aspects.

The time invested in training is not wasted. Instead, it will help you to reduce future stress and time-wasting. The difference between an expert and a rookie is knowledge and experience. When you don't know how to do something, it will look like the hardest thing on earth. On the other hand, once you know what to do, it becomes ridiculously simple.

Get The Right Tool

Using the right tool is like a square peg in a square hole – it fits perfectly. Even if you have the training and skills required to carry out a task, you will still struggle when you don't have the right tools. If you try to use a knife to cut down a tree, you will make progress if you are persistent enough, but it will take months, if not years before you can achieve that task.

However, when you get a chain saw machine, you can even cut down multiple trees in a day. You don't have to keep doing things the traditional way. Always seek faster and more efficient ways to do things to save time and energy. Investing in a machine or device that can make your work faster, is a smart decision. A simple Internet search can help you to find devices and machines that can help you simplify challenging tasks.

Get Mentorship

It is not everything you have to experience in life, before you learn. You can take advantage of the experience and knowledge of others, to move faster in life. A mentor can give you ten years of experience that can make you achieve something five years faster than you would have done it. Never underrate the place of a mentor, especially when the person has your interest at heart.

A mentor in a field knows most of the pitfalls that can derail your progress. Therefore, he or she will warn you ahead, so that you can be more careful to avoid them. You shouldn't be afraid to make a mistake. Yet, you can reduce the chances of committing errors when you have people that have gone ahead, to help you. There are always people that have achieved whatever you want to achieve in life. Find them and learn from them to save time.

Personal Honesty

You might deceive others, but you should always be honest with yourself. One of the reasons people waste time is that they embark on projects that do not suit their characteristics. You don't have to do everything that is offered to you. You should be honest enough to admit when you realize that another person is more suitable for a role. It is not every opportunity you have to accept.

If you are given a leadership role and you know that you don't have what it takes to function effectively in that office, respectfully decline it. Keep improving yourself until you are ready to handle that kind of responsibility. If you embark on projects that are beyond your current level, you would mess things up and people would mock you for being an abject failure. Don't let the hype of people get into your head. Some people would push you to accept a responsibility, simply so that they can watch you fail.

Hire An Expert

A part of personal honesty is knowing when you should hire an expert. It is not everything that you are capable of doing. Once you notice that you don't have the skills to get something done, get more training or hire an expert. Trying to do something you don't have the ability to achieve, will lead to time-wasting and it can also aggravate a problem. One of the best things you can do, to save time and energy, is to call for help when necessary.

By watching the expert, you can also learn how to fix the same problem the next time. It is possible that what should be fixed is not a serious issue. Still, it is better to seek the help of a professional, than experiment with the issue and make it more complicated. This is the reason some people lose their lives. Instead of seeking the help of a doctor, they resort to self-medication, which makes the situation worse and even makes it too late to call a professional.

Chapter Five: Time-Management Hacks

This book will not be complete if we don't talk about time management. Learning to be an effective time-keeper is the beginning of living an impactful and purposeful life. Some people keep claiming that they don't have enough time to carry out their daily tasks. Some people would even wish that they have more than twenty-four hours a day. The issue is never that you don't have enough time. Rather, it is because you need to improve your time-management skills. The following tips will help you in this regard.

Declutter Your Schedule

The quality of your decision-making is a crucial factor that determines how you spend your time. Sometimes, the reason you don't have enough time for the things that matter to you, is that you spend time on the things that matter little to your long-term plans. For example, you might be volunteering or participating in activities that will matter little to you in the long run. When I was in college, I was an active member of my department's football team and I also played an active part in class politics.

At some point, I had to ask myself how these activities would contribute to my future. I had to ask myself these questions because my commitment to these activities was beginning to affect my academic performance. Besides, they didn't allow me to spend time acquiring skills that could add more value to my life. I love football but I am convinced that I don't intend to be a footballer. So, I have to just play football whenever I am free instead of something I did seriously, like before. This decision allowed me to create more time for other things that I would need in the future.

Create A Road Map

Once you declutter your schedule by eliminating the activities that don't mean so much to you, you are ready to create a plan that would accommodate the tasks that are more relevant to you. Start the day with a plan of the tasks you want to achieve for that day. This would give you a clear view of what you need to do, at certain points of the day. This would also make it easier for you to eliminate distractions and keep your focus.

When you don't have a clear plan for your day, anything can come in. Whether you spend your day wisely or not, you will end up spending it on something. So, to avoid wasting so many heartbeats, ensure that you have a plan for the day. It is even possible to have plans for a week or even a month.

Set Boundaries

When you have a clear plan for your day or week, no one will be able to drag you into something irrelevant. A plan ensures that you can tell others that you have things slated out for certain periods of the day. If you don't have a plan for your day, others will drag you into their plans. You don't have to lie to the people around you to avoid them making you do things that you don't want to do.

Instead, create a plan for your day. Let the people around you know that you are a busy person that has plans for his or her life. When they see you this way, they will value your presence more. They will see the time you choose to spend with them as something valuable they should treasure. When you don't set boundaries, people would waste your time and all you would have to show for it is regret.

Delegate When Necessary

You cannot achieve so much, in this time-limited world, if you are the one that does everything you need to do. If you are a career parent, you have a lot of responsibilities that are all important. Sometimes, you want to cook, do your laundry, do your hair, get items in the mall, help your kids with their assignments, and work in your office, all in one day! The thought of all these activities can be so overwhelming, that you might have emotional and physical exhaustion.

Instead of trying to do all of these things by yourself, you can buy yourself time by asking for help. If your kids are old enough, let them help out with some things at home. If you are not a single parent, your spouse can also help out. If it is all too much and you don't have anyone you can trust to help you, you can employ a house help to reduce the stress.

Limit Experimentation

You should be open to experiences. Yet, you need to reduce the tendency to experiment because you don't have all the time in the world. Find a way that is effective to carry out all your daily tasks and stick to it. If you find a better way to do them, integrate the techniques but you cannot afford to be chopping and changing things, incessantly. Young people are fond of this. They experiment with almost everything, including relationships and careers.

This approach will make you incapable of settling with anything or anyone. You should not date people, just to find out whether it will work out or not. Instead, take your time to study the person as a friend. Notice his or her strengths and weaknesses, during the moments he or she is not likely to be putting up a performance to impress you. Ensure that the benefits far outweigh the limitations, before you commit to a relationship, to avoid wasting your time with different people.

Reduce Interruptions

There are times that certain things interrupt your plans unexpectedly. Life can just be like that, sometimes. Yet, there are times that these interruptions came because you didn't plan ahead. For example, you cannot plan for the death of a loved one, which might alter your plans or even make you abandon them altogether. However, you can choose to switch off your phone or put it on silent, so that you don't have distractions while trying to complete a task. Remember that every second counts. So, plan for things that can affect your momentum or reduce your engagement.

Avoid MultiTasking

The human mind is not designed to do several things at the same time. When you try to do more than one thing at a time, it will reduce your productivity and might lead to time-wasting. As much as possible, try to focus on one thing at a time. I mentioned this earlier. This is what mindfulness is all about. As much as possible, design your schedule in such a way that you would only have to focus on one thing -at a time. Multi-tasking is neither good for your health or your efficiency. A Bryan College study confirmed this.

Chapter Six: How To Achieve Work-Life Balance

It is said that many people spend so much time trying to earn money that they fail in the other crucial aspects of their lives. There are other essential areas of your life that you must not neglect. If not, you might never use more than half of the available two billion heartbeats, before you die. In this chapter, we will explore how you can spend your time, wisely, by investing in your health and your interpersonal relationships.

Health Is Wealth

Your health is one of your greatest treasures. Sadly, many people never realize its importance until they lose it. It is expected that you give it your all to achieve your dreams and become successful in life. However, the big question is what is the essence of earning so much money, accolades, and awards when you cannot enjoy it in good health? It doesn't make any sense. It is even better to have just enough that you can enjoy while in good health.

Your health is too much to sacrifice for success in your career. This is the reason so many successful people spend millions of dollars every year on hospital bills. Some of them didn't respect basic health principles while chasing success. By the time they achieve wealth and fame, their health is already failing. This doesn't mean that you shouldn't give it your best to get to the top of your career. Yet, if it will make you lose your health, it is not worth it.

Note that health is not only physical. Your mental and social well-being are also parts of your overall health. You have to pay attention to every aspect of your health while striving to earn as much as possible and achieve success in life. If you fail to take care of your health, your body will start malfunctioning and this could lead to an early grave. Time invested in taking care of your health can buy you more heartbeats.

The Value Of Relationships

There is nothing wrong with thinking about how you can do what is best for you. Yet, you are a selfish person if all you think about is yourself. If you don't value your relationships, by the time your two billion heartbeats begin to count down towards the end, you will be full of regrets. Many people on their sickbed wish that they spent more time with their family and the people that matter to them. If you are not careful, the desire to make money can make you so engrossed that you will sideline your interpersonal relationships.

Just like your health, you should never neglect your interpersonal relationships. Success is only worth it when you have people that can enjoy it with you. You should want your friends and family to be there on those days you reach certain milestones in your life. On those days, when you look around and discover that your friends and family are absent, it dampens the achievement. There are situations where people cry when they realize that the people that matter to them, were not there to witness their greatness.

Therefore, you should never sacrifice your interpersonal relationships for wealth and fame. Let them grow with you and witness your greatness. It can be lonely at the top, when you don't have people that truly care about you, around you. Many celebrities battle depression because they find it difficult to find true and loyal friends around them. Many of the people around them are gold diggers and this makes it difficult for them to trust others.

Balance Is Key

What you need is balance because you need to strive to achieve success in life. You will have to take risks to achieve relevance in life. You cannot be happy without a sense of achievement. So, it would be ridiculous to suggest that you should protect your health and family in such a way that will prevent you from fulfilling your potential. There is a lot to be explored in this world and you will have yourself to blame if you don't strive for excellence because you are afraid that it might affect your health and relationship with your loved ones.

You should just know your priorities. Your health and your interpersonal relationships should be your priority. It is possible to maintain your health and have a wonderful family, while striving for success. There are many celebrities in the world today that have a close bond with their family and maintain physical fitness. So, it is achievable.

What they have learned is to bring balance into their professional and personal life. They know what matters the most but it has not stopped them from working hard to earn success and fame. Let such people be your example. Find out how they were able to do it and learn from their blueprint for work-life balance.

Work-Life Balance Hacks

For you to live happily, a work-life balance is not negotiable. The following tips will help you in this regard:

No Interference Policy

Many people have a culture of letting their family struggles affect their performance at work and vice versa. It is never easy. Still, if you want to enjoy a work-life balance, you need to avoid letting your job stress affect how you relate with your family. On the other hand, ensure you focus when you are working, even when there is an issue to be taken care of. If possible, take time off from your work to deal with your family issues. Interference on both sides will never end well for you.

Separate Work From Relationships

Your loved ones cannot be pleased with you when you have a culture of working when you are with them. It can ruin your marriage when you are always talking to a client whenever you plan to spend time together with your spouse. You should not act in a way that will make your spouse think that you value your job more than him or her. Try, as much as possible, to let your office tasks stay in the office. It can strain your interpersonal relationships when you work at home. Even if you are a remote worker, ensure that you have a workspace.

Carry Your Family Along

There is no doubt that your job might be demanding. Yet, you must not lose your family because of it. You can get a new job if you lose one, but you cannot replace your loved ones if you lose them. Your family and friends will be proud of you when you are diligent at your work.

However, they don't want to feel that you value your job more than them. As much as possible, let them know what you are doing and what you need to do. This will help them to know when to leave you alone to focus on a task, and when to support you when necessary.

Chapter Seven: Recovering From Setbacks

Getting stuck in the past can make you miserable for the rest of your life. There is no doubt that there are some situations that can be devastating. Yet, nothing in your past should be strong enough to determine or ruin your future. If you want to make the most of your two billion heartbeats, you must learn to recover from setbacks as fast as possible. The following tips will help you to become a resilient individual.

You Cannot Turn Back The Hands Of Time

The first thing you need to realize after suffering a setback, is that you cannot turn back the hands of time. Many songs and movies have been written about the possibility of going back on a time machine to right our wrongs, but such a possibility is only in the realm of imagination. In reality, it is not possible. You cannot bring your loved ones from the grave again, and you cannot change whatever happened in the past.

What you have now, are today and the future. So, you should concentrate your efforts on making the right choices, today. There might be days that the mistakes you made in the past would come back to haunt you, but don't read too much into them. Take responsibility for your actions and don't be afraid of their consequences. Keep your head up. That is the only way you can make the remaining heartbeats the best possible, in your lifetime.

Forgive And Let Go

One of the reasons people struggle to let go of the past is that they struggle to forgive others and themselves. Remember that your annoyance and sadness cannot change what you have done. If you need to apologize to anyone who was hurt by your actions, do it. Even if they refuse to forgive you, move on. If you keep making the right choices, they may find reasons to forgive you over time.

If you don't forgive yourself and others that hurt you, it can lead to the development of harmful habits, such as heavy drinking and irresponsible partying. You cannot afford to squander the remaining heartbeats you have, on regrets because of what you did in the past. If you move on, you might not be proud of the mistakes you made in the past but you will be proud of yourself for turning it around.

The Future Offers New Opportunities

It is true that no human being is certain about what the future holds. Yet, we can be sure that it offers us the opportunity to make better choices. You might have hurt your spouse and ruined your marriage but that doesn't mean that your marital story should end that way. You might not be able to get your spouse back again, but you can still have a successful marriage with someone else, if you don't give up on yourself.

In the same way, you might have lost your dream job because of carelessness and bad habits. Still, that doesn't mean that you cannot get another job in the future. In fact, there have been many celebrities that have gone on to become success stories after they were sacked. Steve Jobs and J.K. Rowling are sterling examples, in this regard. J.K. Rowling was sacked because she was writing stories at work. However, this eventually became a blessing in disguise for her. It gave her the time to concentrate on writing *Harry Potter*, which is a multi-billion-dollar success.

Never Give Up

Giving up should never be part of the options you have when you suffer a setback. You should never get to that point where you feel that you don't have hope again.

Whatever has happened to you, has also happened to other people before. Don't let negative thoughts overwhelm you. It is true that you could have done better but you didn't. You still have the time to rewrite your story if only you will not give up on yourself.

Focus On What You Can Control

Many people overwhelm themselves with negative thoughts because they focus on the things they cannot control while neglecting the things they can . You don't have control over the past. So, concentrating on it is pointless. In the same way, you have little control over the future, which makes anxiety a total waste of time. Instead of slating yourself for your past mistakes, why not work towards making better choices today?

In the same way, it is pointless to be worried about the possibility of repeating the same mistakes in the future. Learn from your past because it is a sign of intelligence. If you don't learn from your mistakes, you might repeat them in the future. As long as you understand why things didn't work out in the past, you are prepared to avoid falling into the same trap in the future.

Have Internal Locus Of Control

Your locus of control is how you appropriate the things that happen to you. If you have a culture of putting the blame on others or situations when things are not going your way, you have an external locus of control. On the other hand, when you take responsibility for your failures, you have an internal locus of control. An external locus of control will not let you improve when necessary.

On the other hand, an internal locus of control will make you look at the role you played in your failure, which will help you make amends. For example, if a person that has an external locus of control loses a job, he will blame it on his boss or his family issues. However, a person that has an internal locus of control will evaluate his performance and how he could have handled the situation in a better way.

Avoid Negative People

Negative people can make you get stuck in your past. They would keep reminding you about your failures. Such people act this way due to various reasons. Sometimes, they remind you about your past because they don't want you to achieve the same level of success they possess. This is often the case when you are their competitor for a position.

Don't allow the words of such people to affect you. Some people would criticize you because they are afraid of your potential to achieve more success than them. Stay away from such people. Whenever you are trying to recover from a setback, try to find people that have gone through the same situation before, that turned it around. Let their stories inspire you to turn things around.

Chapter Eight: Gratitude All The Way

What you will discover, as you keep growing, is that life does not always give you what you want and deserve. Yet, you cannot afford to waste time thinking about the things that never went your way. One of the ways you can ensure that you make every second count, is to maintain an attitude of gratitude.

Make Gratitude Your Default Thinking

The default thinking of most people is negative thoughts. They are almost like the character that plays Joker in Batman movies. Even when they have positive events happening around them, they tend to focus on the negative aspects of it. For example, instead of celebrating their promotion, they are still sad that they are not earning as much as a friend. They are not happy that their spouse is not as romantic as their friend's partner. This mindset is not healthy for you. It will fill your life with dark and hurtful thoughts.

Instead, you can switch to the other mode. You can choose to make gratitude your default thinking. You can be grateful, even for what is happening in the lives of others. When this is absent, you will be jealous of your friends and family. Instead of celebrating when they achieve a milestone, you will find a way to talk down on their success. Instead of praising them for working hard to get to a new level, you will accrue their success to luck. When people notice that you have this kind of attitude, they will start avoiding you.

Count Your Blessings

Many of us never realize how blessed and privileged we are because of the tendency to focus on the negatives. Life always gives us both sides of the divide. There are times that things will work the way you want them to, and there will also be days things won't go your way at all. It is on those sad days that you need to practice gratitude. Anyone can be happy when things are going smoothly, but it takes a resilient person to find reasons to be glad when things are not going well.

Life can be tough and you need to develop a thick skin to weather the storm. During the days things are not going as planned, you need to count your blessings. This is the way to ensure that you are not overwhelmed by negative emotions. You are responsible for your happiness. You can refuse to be a victim of circumstances. This is the reason the same thing happens to two different people and one commits suicide while the other forges ahead.

Remain Optimistic

Contrary to popular opinion, optimism is not the opposite of realism. The fact that you are optimistic doesn't mean that you are not realistic. It is okay to have a realistic expectation of your chances of success. Still, you have to expect things to work out well for you. Optimism gives you the necessary motivation to keep pushing and working towards a goal. In the name of realism, some people would want to cut their losses, in case things don't work well, which makes them do less than their ability.

In a time-limited world, you should always give your best, whenever you are involved in anything. If you know that you don't want to go all out to achieve something, you should avoid it altogether. Whatever is worth doing in the first place is worth doing with the whole of your energy. Even if things don't work out eventually, you should be proud of yourself when you gave it your all.

Surround Yourself With Positive People

I mentioned earlier that you should avoid negative people. Yet, it is only one side of the coin. It is not complete until you also surround yourself with positive people. You don't need to stay around negative people to have negative thoughts. Your inner critic can generate negative energy and ruin your mood. So, it is vital that you have the right people around you. You need such people, especially on those days that things didn't go your way.

They will give you the emotional support that will help you to remind yourself about the positive sides of the unpleasant experience. Positive people have a culture of looking at the bright side of a negative situation while negative people have a knack for finding the downsides of a positive situation. So, when you have positive people around you, it will be easier for you to consider the positive aspects of an incident regardless of how terrible it seems.

Leverage Journaling

One of the most effective ways you can practice gratitude is by taking advantage of journaling. Studies have proven that journaling has several benefits, such as stress reduction and improvement of mood. So, when you practice gratitude by leveraging journaling, you are combining the impacts and benefits of these two practices. The key thing about journaling is documenting your experiences. It is an effective way to relieve stress and improve your performance.

If you are feeling like life has not been fair to you, pick up your journal and list out all the things in your life that you are grateful for. This practice will remind you about all the positive things in your life. As you do this, you will realize that you will start generating positive emotions that will improve your mood. You can practice journaling with a book or on your digital devices. Just choose an option that is the most suitable for you.

Be Your Number One Fan

If you don't rate yourself, don't expect others to do so. It is good to have a sincere and objective evaluation of yourself. Yet, you should never lose your self-confidence in anything. If you feel that there are areas of your life you need to improve, work on them. Sharpen your skills when necessary, and read books that can help you improve certain aspects of your life.

Never stop believing in yourself. When you don't value yourself, it will be difficult for you to practice gratitude. You will be overwhelmed by the thoughts of your weaknesses in such a way that you will overlook or downplay your strengths. We all have areas of our lives that we don't want others to know about. So, you shouldn't think it is strange when you notice that you have deficiencies. Improve when necessary and accept the ones you cannot change.

Conclusion

At the beginning of this journey, I stated that the fact we have just around two billion heartbeats as humans, could either scare you or motivate you to make the best out of your life. I believe that it should have the latter effect by now and not the former. You have to accept this reality and let it give you the momentum to make every second count. We discussed goal setting, work-life balance, resilience, eliminating procrastination, time-management hacks, and practicing gratitude.

If you leverage the tips that were given in each of the chapters of this book, you are on the right path to becoming a well-rounded individual. They will give you the discipline to avoid wasting time, while helping you to enjoy every aspect of your life to the fullest. The choices you make today will determine how you will end your life. This book has given you the information needed to make quality choices. Don't waste it.

Thank you for reading this book!

If you found this book helpful, I would be grateful if you would **post an honest review on Amazon** so this book can reach other supportive readers like you!

All you need to do is digitally flip to the back and leave your review. Or visit amazon.com/author/senseipauldavid click the correct book cover and click on the blue link next to the yellow stars that says, "customer reviews."

As always...

It's a great day to be alive!

Get/Share Our FREE All-Ages Mental Health Books Now!

FREE Self-Development Book for Every Family

senseiselfdevelopment.senseipublishing.com

Click Below or Search Amazon for Another Book In Each Series Or Visit:

www.amazon.com/author/senseipauldavid

Check out our **recommendations** for other books for adults & kids plus other great resources by visiting
www.senseipublishing.com/resources/

Join Our Publishing Journey!

If you would like to receive FREE BOOKS, special offers, please visit www.senseipublishing.com and join our newsletter by entering your email address in the pop-up box

Follow Our Engaging Blog NOW! senseipauldavid.ca

FREE Self-Development Book
senseiselfdevelopment.senseipublishing.com

FREE BONUS!!!
Experience Over 25 FREE Engaging Guided Meditations!

Prized Skills & Practices for Adults & Kids.
Help Restore Deep-Sleep, Lower Stress,
Improve Posture, Navigate Uncertainty &
More.

Download the Free Insight Timer App
and click the link below:
http://insig.ht/sensei_paul

If you like these meditations & want to go
deeper email me for a FREE 30min LIVE
Coaching Session:
senseipauldavid@senseipublishing.com

About Sensei Publishing

Sensei Publishing commits itself to help people of all ages transform into better versions of themselves by providing high-quality and research-based self-development books with an emphasis on mental health and guided meditations. Sensei Publishing offers well-written e-books, audiobooks, paperbacks and online courses that simplify complicated but practical topics in line with its mission to inspire people towards positive transformation.

It's a great day to be alive!

About the Author

I create simple & transformative eBooks & Guided Meditations for Adults & Children proven to help navigate uncertainty, solve niche problems & bring families closer together.

I'm a former finance project manager, private pilot, jiu-jitsu instructor, musician & former University of Toronto Fitness Trainer. I prefer a science-based approach to focus on these & other areas in my life to stay humble & hungry to evolve. I hope you enjoy my work and I'd love to hear your feedback.

- It's a great day to be alive!
Sensei Paul David

Scan & Follow/Like/Subscribe:
Facebook, Instagram, YouTube:
@senseipublishing

Scan using your phone/iPad camera for Social Media Visit us at www.senseipublishing.com and sign up to our newsletter to learn more about our exciting books and to experience our FREE Guided Meditations for Kids & Adults.

www.ingramcontent.com/pod-product-compliance
Lightning Source LLC
Chambersburg PA
CBHW011929050726
47591CB00009B/2401